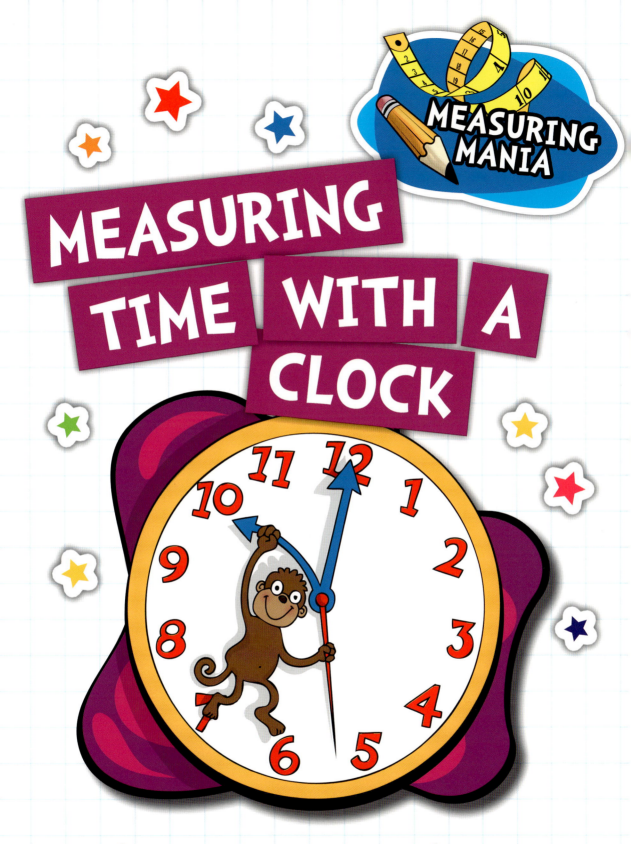

MEASURING MANIA

MEASURING TIME WITH A CLOCK

by Beth Bence Reinke   illustrated by Kathleen Petelinsek

Published in the United States of America by Cherry Lake Publishing
Ann Arbor, Michigan
www.cherrylakepublishing.com

Consultants: Janice Bradley, PhD, Mathematically Connected Communities,
New Mexico State University; Marla Conn, ReadAbility, Inc.

Editorial direction: Red Line Editorial
Book design and illustration: The Design Lab

Photo credits: Tatyana Vyc/Shutterstock Images, 4, 13; Shutterstock Images, 6,
12, 14, 16, 18, 21; Hung Chung Chih/Shutterstock Images, 17

Library of Congress Cataloging-in-Publication Data
Reinke, Beth Bence, author.
  Measuring time with a clock / Beth Bence Reinke.
     pages cm. — (Measuring mania)
  Audience: 5–8.
  Audience: K to grade 3.
  Includes bibliographical references and index.
  ISBN 978-1-62431-650-0 (hardcover) — ISBN 978-1-62431-677-7 (pbk.) —
ISBN 978-1-62431-704-0 (pdf) — ISBN 978-1-62431-731-6 (hosted ebook)
  1. Time measurements—Juvenile literature. 2. Clocks and watches—Juvenile
literature. I. Title.

  QB213.R45 2014
  529'.7–dc23
                              2013029074

Cherry Lake Publishing would like to acknowledge
the work of The Partnership for 21st Century Skills.
Please visit www.p21.org for more information.

Printed in the United States of America
Corporate Graphics Inc.
January 2014

Table of Contents

CHAPTER ONE

Clocks with Hands and Clocks with Numbers

BUZZ BUZZ

7:00

What time do you wake up for school?

Buzz, buzz, goes Kate's alarm clock. Time to get up! Kate needs to get ready. The school bus will come in half an hour. How many minutes are in half an hour? Measuring time on a clock will help you find out.

Clocks with faces and hands are called **analog** clocks. **Digital** clocks have only numbers. Look around. What kinds of clocks do you see?

The clock on the wall is analog. The clock on the microwave is digital.

Measuring time helps us keep track of when things happen. What time does the ball game start? How many minutes of recess are left? When is lunchtime?

It helps us know how long things take, too. How many minutes do the cookies bake? How long will you brush your teeth? Let's measure time!

Brush your teeth twice a day. And brush for at least two minutes!

To do the activities in this book, you will need:

- paper plates
- paper fasteners
- card stock paper
- markers
- scissors
- index cards

Gather what you need.

CHAPTER TWO

Units of Time

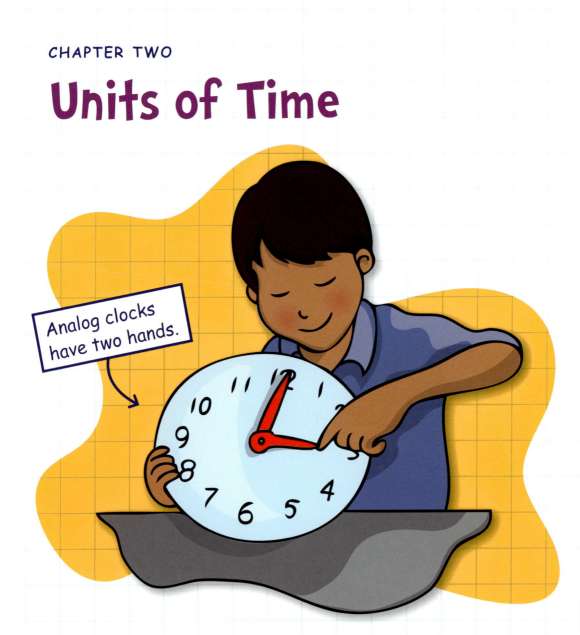

Analog clocks have two hands.

Juan is making clocks in math class. Each analog clock has two hands. The little hand points to the hour. The big hand shows the minutes. Hours and minutes are **units** for measuring time.

There are 60 minutes in one hour. But a clock face has only 12 numbers. On a clock, there are five minutes between each number. How many five-minute blocks are in one hour?

Some clocks show seconds. There are 60 seconds in a minute. The second hand moves really fast!

When the minute hand moves from 12 to 1, 5 minutes have passed.

Math class is over at nine o'clock. The hour hand points to 9. The minute hand is at 12.

A digital clock shows 9:00. That is another way to say nine o'clock. The hour is on the left of the colon. The minutes are on the right.

Recess begins at 1:00. Kate and Juan play outside for half an hour. The minute hand moves halfway around the clock to the 6. Recess ends at 1:30.

In half an hour, the minute hand moves halfway around the clock. Here it moved from the 12 to the 6.

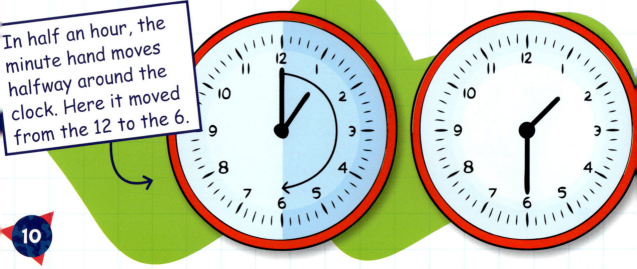

Make Your Own Clock

You can make a clock, too. You can practice telling time.

INSTRUCTIONS:
1. Write the numbers 1 through 12 around the edge of a paper plate.
2. Cut out two hands from card stock paper. Make one hand long and the other short.
3. Poke a hole in one end of each hand. Attach them to the center of the clock with a fastener.
4. Now you can practice. Set the clock to 9:00. Now try 12:00 and 1:30. It's fun to move the hands, isn't it?
5. Practice showing time on the hour. Here are examples: 3:00, 4:00, and 8:00.
6. Now try time on the half hour. Try 2:30, 5:30, and 10:30. Keep practicing!

To get a copy of this activity, visit www.cherrylakepublishing.com/activities.

There are 5 minutes for each number you write on your clock.

CHAPTER THREE

How Long Does It Take?

In one hour, the short hand moves forward one number on the clock.

Juan rides his bike for an hour. One hour is 60 minutes. The hour hand moves from one number to the next. Juan starts riding at 4:00. What time is he finished? If you said 5:00, you're right.

Kate reads a book for half an hour. Half an hour is 30 minutes. Kate reads from 6:00 to 6:30. At 6:30, the long hand points to the 6.

The big hand moves 30 minutes when it moves from 12 to 6.

Juan's cookies need to bake for ten minutes. It takes five minutes for the minute hand to move from one number to the next.

The minute hand is on the 12. Juan puts the cookies in the oven. He counts the minutes: 1, 2, 3, 4, 5. The minute hand is on the 1 after five minutes. He counts 6, 7, 8, 9, 10. After ten minutes, the minute hand is on the 2. The cookies are done. Yum!

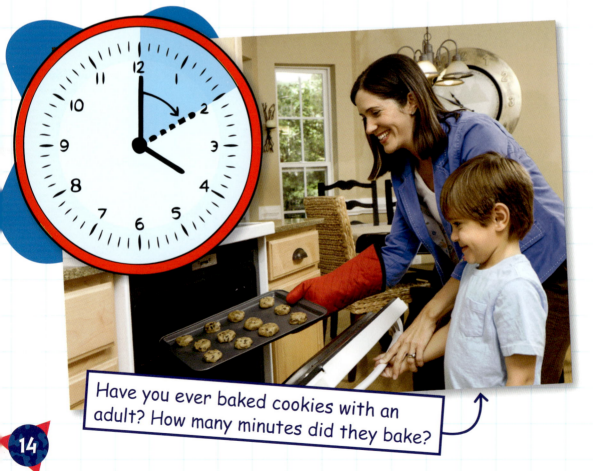

Have you ever baked cookies with an adult? How many minutes did they bake?

Measuring Time by Fives

There are five minutes between numbers on the clock. Practice measuring time by five minutes. Use your practice clock from the first activity.

INSTRUCTIONS:
1. Think of things that take you 5, 10, 15, 20, or 30 minutes to do.
2. Write them on index cards.
3. Shuffle the cards. Put them face down in a pile.
4. Choose a card. Move your clock hands that many minutes.
5. Keep practicing until all the cards are done.

To get a copy of this activity, visit www.cherrylakepublishing.com/activities.

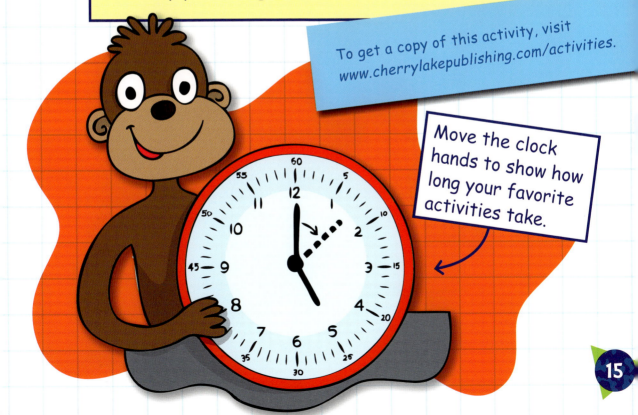

Move the clock hands to show how long your favorite activities take.

CHAPTER FOUR

A Time for Every Activity

There are 24 hours in one day. This means the little hand points to each number on the clock twice a day. There is nine o'clock each morning and again each evening. We use **a.m.** and **p.m.** to tell them apart. We use a.m. when a time is between **midnight** and **noon**.

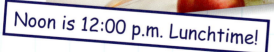

Noon is 12:00 p.m. Lunchtime!

Midnight is 12:00 a.m. You are asleep!

We use p.m. for times between noon and midnight. At twelve o'clock noon, it is lunchtime! At twelve o'clock midnight, it is dark. You're asleep at midnight.

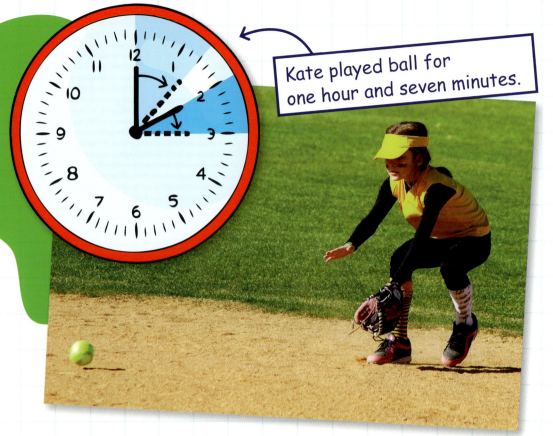

Kate played ball for one hour and seven minutes.

Kate has softball practice on Saturday at 2:00. Today practice ended at 3:07. How long did Kate play ball? She uses the clock hands to figure it out.

It takes 12 minutes to walk home from the ball field. If Kate leaves the ball field at 3:15, what time will she get home? If you said 3:27, you're right!

eat lunch

2:30 p.m.

Match That Time!

Juan and Kate made a matching game. You can make your own game, too. Grab a friend and play together. Match the activities to the correct time.

INSTRUCTIONS:
1. Write activities on index cards.
2. Write the time when you do each activity on different cards.
3. Shuffle the activity cards. Put them facedown in one pile.
4. Lay out the time cards faceup.
5. To play, take turns pulling out an activity card. Find the time card that matches that activity.
6. You can use these activities and times or make up your own. Have fun!

To get a copy of this activity, visit www.cherrylakepublishing.com/activities.

eat breakfast

7:15 a.m.

put on your pajamas

take an afternoon nap

sleep

8:15 p.m.

12:00 a.m. (midnight)

12:00 p.m. (noon)

CHAPTER FIVE

You Can Measure Time

How many clocks can you find in your home?

Clocks are everywhere. They're on the wall and in cell phones. Clocks are even in cars. People use clocks to measure time every day. Now you can, too!

Here are more fun ways to measure time:

- Draw two clocks on a piece of paper. Make one clock show your bedtime. Make the other clock show what time you get up. How many hours do you sleep?
- Look at the time on a digital clock. Draw an analog clock with the same time.
- Time how long it takes to do things. Some ideas are: brush your teeth, go grocery shopping, visit the library, clean your room, color a picture.
- Count the clocks in your home. Which one do you use the most?

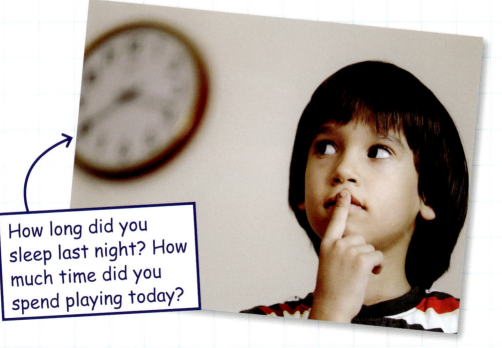

How long did you sleep last night? How much time did you spend playing today?

Glossary

a.m. (AY-ehm) before noon; between midnight and noon

analog (AN-uh-log) a type of clock with a face and hands

digital (DIJ-i-tuhl) a type of clock with numbers separated by a colon

midnight (MID-nyt) twelve o'clock at nighttime

noon (noon) twelve o'clock in the daytime

p.m. (PEE-ehm) after noon; between noon and midnight

units (YOO-nits) standard amounts that are used to measure things

For More Information

BOOKS

King, Andrew. *Measuring Weight and Time*. Brookfield, CT: Copper Beech Books, 2002.

Vogel, Julia. *Measuring Time: The Clock*. Mankato, MN: The Child's World, 2013.

WEB SITES

Enchanted Learning—Clock Craft

http://www.enchantedlearning.com/crafts/clocks/clock/index.shtml
Print out a pattern of a clock and its hour and minute hands. Make your own clock to practice telling time.

Math is Fun—Fun with Analog and Digital Clocks

http://www.mathsisfun.com/time-clocks-analog-digital.html
Change the time on the clocks by moving the hands or using the buttons.

Index

About the Author

Beth Bence Reinke has degrees in biology and nutrition. She is a registered dietitian, children's author, and a columnist for her favorite sport, NASCAR. Beth enjoys watching race cars make a lap around the track in less than a minute. Her favorite time on the digital clock is 11:11.